Original title:

Knotted Wreaths Inside the Mermaid Hack

Author: Olivia Oja

ISBN HARDBACK: 978-1-80562-447-9

ISBN PAPERBACK: 978-1-80563-968-8

Interlaced Dreams of the Aqua Realm

In the depths where shadows play,
Aqua visions swirl and sway,
Mystic whispers fill the air,
Each dream a tale, a hidden prayer.

Beneath the waves, secrets lie,
Dancing pearls, like stars in sky,
Tides of time, they ebb and flow,
Guiding hearts where none may go.

Glowing corals, vibrant and bright,
Illuminate the dark of night,
Lost in beauty, longing to roam,
Aqua realm, forever our home.

Mermaids sing with voices pure,
Enchanting all, their magic sure,
Every ripple, a story spun,
In the Aqua Realm, dreams have begun.

The Dance of Lost Nautical Nostalgia

Waves that crash, a haunting sound,
Echoes of a past unbound,
Sails unfurl with tales to tell,
In the dance where memories dwell.

Glistening foam, a dreamy sight,
Guides the lost through realms of night,
Footsteps trail on sands of time,
Lost nautical, a rhythm sublime.

Old shipwrecks whisper stories grand,
In the silence, a patient hand,
Caught in nets of ebb and flow,
Where the tides of longing grow.

Faded maps and forgotten lore,
Chart the paths to distant shore,
Yearning hearts find solace here,
In the dance, we conquer fear.

Woven Notes of a Waterbound Heart

Flowing rivers sing a tune,
Beneath the gaze of silver moon,
Each note a pulse of gentle grace,
In the currents, our dreams embrace.

Woven tales of whispers soft,
Carry hopes, like leaves aloft,
Every drop a precious part,
Melodies from the waterbound heart.

Stillness wraps the twilight air,
As echoes fade, we stop and stare,
Finding peace in nature's art,
Where the sky meets the ocean's heart.

In harmony, we drift along,
Every wave sings a tender song,
Water's touch, a sweet caress,
In its depths, we find our rest.

The Siren's Tapestry of Longing

Amongst the rocks, a voice so clear,
A siren's song, both sweet and near,
Woven threads of love and pain,
In each note, a heart's refrain.

Golden strands of sunlight weave,
In the ocean's arms, we believe,
Longing lingers in the tide,
In the depths, our dreams collide.

Fingers brush the silken waves,
Tracing paths where memory saves,
Each pulse a promise, soft yet stark,
In the tapestry, love leaves its mark.

Call of the sea, we can't resist,
Daring hearts drawn to the mist,
Siren's call, forever true,
In the deep, we find our due.

The Sea's Labyrinth of Entrapment

In the depths where shadows linger,
Waves whisper tales of those who roam.
Currents twist with secret fingers,
Binding hearts to ocean's home.

A ship sails forth through misty veils,
Chasing dreams beneath the foam.
Yet dangers weave through briny trails,
And lead the lost far from their home.

Ghostly lights flicker in the haze,
Luring sailors to the rocks.
In the labyrinth, time decays,
While fate awaits in tangled locks.

Echoes laugh in watery chambers,
Resonating like forgotten songs.
Each turn unveils both joy and dangers,
As the ocean's grip grows ever strong.

But mariners brave with spirits bold,
Seek the truth beneath the waves.
For even the sea's embrace may hold,
The path to freedom that one craves.

Reveries Entwined with Ocean's Breath

Upon the shore, where dreams take flight,
Whispers dance with salty air.
The sea, a canvas, wild and bright,
Paints stories rich and rare.

Each wave a brushstroke, fresh and clear,
Crafting visions lost to time.
Embraced by rhythm, soft and near,
Hearts pulse in sync with ocean's rhyme.

Reflections shimmer in twilight's glow,
Secrets carried with each tide.
A siren's call, enchanting low,
Lures the dreamers to abide.

In moments spent where sea meets land,
Thoughts drift like shells on sandy beds.
The ocean's breath, a gentle hand,
Unraveling the dreams in our heads.

As stars blink softly in the night,
Beliefs unfurl like sails once furled.
In reveries entwined with ocean's light,
We find ourselves, embraced by the world.

Secrets from a Fathomless Dreamworld

Beneath the waves, where silence dwells,
The fathoms deep hold stories vast.
In whispered echoes, seafarers tell,
Of wonders found and shadows cast.

Anemones sway in the ocean's dance,
Guardians of the secrets old.
In their embrace lies a fleeting chance,
For treasures more precious than gold.

Coral castles, vibrant and grand,
Harbor whispers of lives long past.
Here in the depths, a hidden land,
Where dreams and reality are entwined fast.

Submerged in mysteries, the heart takes flight,
Boundless realms where spirits soar.
In the hush of the deep, bathed in light,
The soul connects forevermore.

With every dive, the truth unfurls,
The ocean's sighs a melody sweet.
Secrets hidden from the world's swirls,
In this dreamworld, hearts and waters meet.

The Mask of the Ocean's Smile

The ocean wears a charming mask,
Beneath its grace, a storm may brew.
In tranquil tides, a hidden task,
As shadows swim where light breaks through.

What mysteries hide in every wave,
As laughter mingles with despair?
The tranquil front that seeks to save,
Masks a tempest lying bare.

Beneath its smile, a turbulent heart,
Rages fierce, yet calm's facade.
For in each swell, a work of art,
Whispers of sorrow, escape unshod.

Yet even within the growing strife,
The sea reveals its tender side.
A cradle for the dreams of life,
Where lovers meet, and time will bide.

So dive beneath the sparkling sheen,
Where all may find their truth revealed.
In every hidden tear, serene,
The ocean's smile, its heart is healed.

Tangled Echoes of Siren Songs

In twilight's glow, they call and sing,
With voices sweet, their magic brings.
Men's hearts are lost in notes so clear,
Drawn closer still, they must not fear.

Beneath the waves, where shadows play,
A haunting dance, they sway, they sway.
A world unseen, where dreams reside,
In tangled echoes, hearts confide.

Yet, caution lies where beauty gleams,
For siren songs weave fragile dreams.
Those who listen find their fate,
In depths where love and danger wait.

Whispers in the Weaving Waves

The ocean whispers soft and low,
Its rhythmic pulse, a timeless flow.
With every tide, a tale unfolds,
Of countless journeys, bright and bold.

In silken strands of seaweed spun,
The tales of old, forever run.
Beneath the moon's illuminating gaze,
The waves embrace in silver plays.

Secrets kept in swirling dance,
Of lost sailors and their romance.
With each crash, a story told,
Of hearts entwined and love so bold.

Secrets of the Ocean's Embrace

In depths where light begins to fade,
The ocean holds its grand parade.
Hidden treasures, lost and found,
In every ripple, life abounds.

Among the corals, colors bright,
Mysteries swim, just out of sight.
Each current whispers, secrets share,
In the ocean's hold, beyond compare.

A lullaby in waves that crash,
Soft serenades in gentle splash.
With every tide, the heart gives chase,
To find the truth in ocean's grace.

Entwined in Salty Currents

Through salty currents, dreams take flight,
Beneath the stars, the world feels right.
The ocean's song, a timeless bond,
That sweeps away the restless dawn.

In every wave, a story breathes,
Full of longing, hopes, and leaves.
With every ebb, the secrets flow,
In tangled paths where lovers go.

The sea's embrace, both fierce and kind,
A dance of souls, forever bind.
In salty tears, they find their place,
Entwined in love, a soft embrace.

Echoes of the Siren's Knot

In twilight's hush, the waters gleam,
Old whispers ride the silver stream.
A siren's call, so soft, so sweet,
Entwined with dreams where shadows meet.

The moonlight weaves a haunting thread,
As secrets swirl where few dare tread.
A phantom voice, both lure and threat,
In echoes lost, the heart is met.

Tangled tales of love and woe,
In depths unseen, where tides do flow.
The deep's embrace, both kind and cruel,
Life's fragile dance, a darkling jewel.

With every wave, a promise made,
A binding sigh, life's charade played.
For in the depths where silence reigns,
Hearts pulse on tides, in hidden chains.

Vows Bound in Seaweed Ribbons

Two souls adrift, in currents bound,
With seaweed ribbons, love is found.
In tangled greens, they pledge their truth,
In whispered vows, the song of youth.

Beneath the swell of ocean's breath,
Their laughter rings, defying death.
Each wave a promise, fierce and strong,
In unison, they weave their song.

The tide ebbs low, yet hearts entwine,
In moonlit glimmers, their love will shine.
For love, like seaweed, bends with grace,
In nature's arms, they find their place.

The ocean's heart beats deep with care,
As currents swirl in tangled hair.
With every rise, with every fall,
Together, they embrace it all.

Entwined Hearts Beneath the Surface

Beneath the waves, where silence dwells,
Two beating hearts weave secret spells.
In watery realms where shadows play,
Love's tender touch will find its way.

Coral gardens, bright and bold,
Hold tales of love, forever told.
In whispered tones, they stitch their fate,
A tapestry of love that won't abate.

The ocean hums a sweet refrain,
In every drop, their joy, their pain.
Entwined together, forever sealed,
Their love a truth, forever revealed.

As storms may rise and tempests roar,
Their bond grows deep, a mighty core.
For in the depths where few may stray,
Their hearts unite, come what may.

The Dance of Murmurs and Twines

In twilight's breath, the waters sigh,
A dance of murmurs, soft and shy.
With every twine, their secrets share,
A fluid ballet, beyond compare.

The surface shimmers with tales untold,
Of lovers' dreams, both brave and bold.
As currents weave through gentle night,
Their spirits soar, a soaring flight.

A waltz of echoes, sweet and light,
Through depths unknown, they chase the night.
For in the sea's embrace, they find,
A solace deep, a love entwined.

With every pulse, the ocean sighs,
As starlit skies twinkle their lies.
Together they twirl in liquid art,
Forever bound, heart to heart.

Reef Reflections on a Tangled Heart

Beneath the waves where shadows dance,
A heart feels lost, yet yearns for chance.
With every ripple, whispers sigh,
A tangled thread, an ocean's cry.

In coral gardens, dreams unfold,
With colors bright, a tale retold.
The sea's embrace, both fierce and kind,
A mirror of what hearts can bind.

As currents pull, the soul must learn,
To navigate both love and yearn.
For in the depths, the truth does swim,
In tangled hearts, the light grows dim.

With every wave, a story spun,
Of fleeting light and shadows run.
In the deep blue, hopes intertwine,
Reflecting fears, the heart must shine.

So listen close to ocean's song,
Your tangled heart can still belong.
In the depths of each embrace,
Find love anew in hidden space.

Moonlit Garlands Across Coral Spires

Under the gaze of silver light,
Coral spires reach for the night.
Moonlit garlands weave a dream,
In the quiet, all things gleam.

The waters ripple with secret tales,
As soft as winds that fill the sails.
Stars above, like jewels bright,
Guide the mariners through the night.

Each bubble formed with every sigh,
Reflects the wishes made on high.
In shimmering hues, the sea's embrace,
Wears the magic of time and space.

Deep below, where shadows play,
Merfolk dance 'neath moon's ballet.
With hearts entwined in silken flows,
The ocean's heartbeat softly glows.

When dawn appears, the spells may fade,
Yet in our dreams, the night won't trade.
For moonlit garlands worn with pride,
Forever bind the ocean wide.

The Merfolk's Secret Tapestry

In hidden depths where secrets weave,
The merfolk craft what hearts believe.
With strands of light and ocean's thread,
A tapestry of dreams is spread.

Each color captures tales of old,
Of bravery and hearts so bold.
In every knot, a wish is known,
A saga of love that's gently sown.

They whisper songs of ancient lore,
Of tides that rise and oceans roar.
In woven patterns, hear the plea,
Of hopes and dreams, eternally free.

Through underwater halls, they glide,
With every stitch, their lives collide.
In laughter and tears, they find their grace,
In secret tapestries, hearts embrace.

For in the depths, they share their art,
Weaving magic with every heart.
The merfolk sing of pathways bright,
As starlit skies give way to light.

Threads of Water and Wonder

From ocean's depths to skies above,
Are threads that bind with kinships of love.
In every drop, a story flows,
Of wonder hidden where no one goes.

Children of the sea, with dreams so vast,
They dance on currents, forever cast.
Each wave a canvas, each tide a chance,
To write a saga in nature's dance.

Where sunlight kisses water's face,
Is magic found in every place.
In the whispers of the seaweed's sway,
Lies the promise of a new day.

Through the bubbles that rise and fall,
Are echoes of nature's timeless call.
Threads of water, threads of light,
Bind the world in pure delight.

So let your heart be open wide,
And ride the tide, let dreams decide.
For in the realms of water's grace,
Wonder awaits in each embrace.

Entangled Hopes Beneath the Sea

In caverns deep where shadows play,
Whispers of dreams wash hopes away.
Coral reefs hold secrets tight,
Guiding lost souls through the night.

Bubbles rise like fleeting thoughts,
Dancing lightly, warmth begot.
Tides that ebb and flow with grace,
Keep the wishes in their place.

A shipwreck's tale of love entwined,
Lingers softly in the brine.
Forgotten vows in salty air,
Echo of hearts that used to care.

Stars above like scattered pearls,
Reflecting hopes in watery swirls.
Every wave a chance reborn,
In ocean's arms, dreams softly mourn.

From depths unknown, enchantments rise,
Brushing whispers through the skies.
Awash in wonder, souls set free,
Beneath the vast, enchanted sea.

Interwoven Horizons of Dreams

In twilight's glow, the world expands,
Where dreams are born from gentle hands.
Fleeting moments blend and weave,
A tapestry of hopes conceived.

Beneath the stars, bright futures dance,
With every heartbeat, a daring chance.
Through tangled paths and winding ways,
Unfold the magic of our days.

Whispers of wind, soft tales unfold,
Of journeys new and tales retold.
Threads of fate in colors bright,
Interweave shadows with the light.

Mountains rise and rivers flow,
Painting horizons in a glow.
Each turn a promise, each step a leap,
In the heart of dreams, our secrets keep.

So let us dance on starlit ground,
In this embrace, our voices found.
Together we'll chase, together we'll gleam,
In the woven tapestry of dream.

Echoing Melodies of Ocean's Heart

With every wave, the ocean sighs,
A symphony beneath the skies.
Melodies born from deep below,
Heartbeats echo in the flow.

Seashells hum forgotten tunes,
Beneath the light of silver moons.
Ebbing rhythms pull and sway,
Guiding lost hearts on their way.

Ocean's whispers in the breeze,
Singing lullabies with ease.
A harmony of ebb and tide,
Where mysteries and dreams reside.

As twilight falls, the waters gleam,
In ocean's arms, we find our dream.
Together, we'll drift through melody,
In every note, a memory.

The echoes call, a sweet refrain,
Binding us through joy and pain.
A tapestry of song and sea,
Where love forever flows, carefree.

Charm in the Current of Time

Beneath the stars, the river winds,
A dance of fate, the heart still binds.
Time flows softly, like a stream,
Carrying wishes, whispers, dreams.

With every turn, a story grows,
In rippling waters, magic flows.
Moments woven, precious and dear,
Enchanted seasons disappear.

From dawn to dusk, the shadows chase,
Moments freeze in time's embrace.
A flicker, a glance, time holds tight,
In this current, hearts take flight.

As clouds drift by in whispered grace,
We find our charm in this sacred space.
Laughter echoes in the unfolding days,
In the river's flow, love finds its ways.

So let us dance on time's soft tide,
With open hearts and dreams inside.
A journey shared, a story told,
In the embrace of time, we behold.

Surreal Patterns of the Aquatic World

Beneath the waves, a dance takes place,
Colors swirl in a fluid embrace.
Rippling hues in a watery gleam,
Every fin and scale a painter's dream.

Anemones sway like dancers in trance,
While schools of fish perform their romance.
In hidden corners of corals bright,
Life unfolds in wondrous delight.

Strange creatures lurk where shadows reside,
In silence they watch, with secrets inside.
On ocean floors where mysteries lie,
The patterns speak softly, as currents sigh.

Deep in the blue, the stories align,
Whispers of treasures, the water's design.
With each ripple, a fresh tale emerges,
In dreams of the deep, the soul gently surges.

The Submerged Labyrinth of Desire

In depths unfathomed, allure does dwell,
A labyrinth woven, a siren's spell.
Tangled paths of shimmering light,
Lead the lost into a dance of the night.

Fluctuating shadows beckon and sway,
As longing hearts drift further away.
An echoing pulse in the ocean's beat,
Each twist a secret, each turn bittersweet.

The ebbing tide tells tales of the past,
Of loves unspoken and dreams that last.
Beneath the foam, desires entwined,
A web of emotions, beautifully defined.

Amidst the coral, hidden truths wait,
In whispers of waters that resonate fate.
In the maze of the deep, brave souls dare,
To seek what is lost, in passions laid bare.

Melodies Entwined in the Seabed's Heart

Soft lullabies drift on the ocean breeze,
As whispers of love float through seaweed trees.
Each bubble a note in a symphony grand,
Echoing softly across the soft sand.

The rhythm of waves, a heart's gentle thrum,
Calls forth the dreams of where we come from.
In caverns of shells, harmonies rise,
Entwined in the heart, where music never dies.

Fishermen's tales, like songs from the heart,
Weave through the tides, each voice plays a part.
With every crest, emotions resound,
In the deepest of oceans, love's magic is found.

From the seabed's embrace, old legends flow,
Of love's sweet refrain, and the longing we know.
As moonlight dances on water's skin,
Melodies of longing, a song we begin.

Fisherman's Knot of Amour

Tied in the twilight with hands of fate,
A fisherman's knot, love's subtle weight.
Bound by the tides and the wind's soft breath,
Entwined with longing, defying death.

Casting nets wide into salt and foam,
The heart's simple catch, forever at home.
With dreams like fish, slippery and bright,
Lurking below in the depths of the night.

Each pull of the line, a story retold,
Of love's fierce grip and the hopes it holds.
In the weave of the rope, connections are made,
A tapestry rich, in the waves that invade.

Through storms and calm, may the lines hold tight,
Fisherman's knot in the soft moonlight.
Together we sail, through tempest and calm,
In the ocean of love, forever our psalm.

The Weaving of Seafoam Wishes

In twilight's glow, the ocean sighs,
With whispers soft, as stars arise.
Each wave a note, in dreams they blend,
A tapestry where hopes ascend.

Fleeting moments, like mist entwined,
In salty breezes, secrets bind.
An echo calls from depths below,
A song of wishes in ebb and flow.

Colors dance on churning tide,
As moonlit paths begin to glide.
The seafoam gathers, a gentle art,
Cocooning wishes, heart to heart.

With every crest, a tale is spun,
Of lovers lost and battles won.
In lullabies of ocean's breath,
We chase the dreams that flutter yet.

So let your heart, like currents roam,
To find the shores that feel like home.
For in each wave, a wish is sewn,
The sea's embrace, where hopes are grown.

Harmonies of the Underwater Bower

Beneath the waves, where shadows play,
An underwater world holds sway.
The coral blooms in twilight's gleam,
Creating harmonies, a dream.

Silken trails of light cascade,
Through kelp and stone, their colors fade.
A gentle symphony of sound,
In depths where ancient tales abound.

The fish join in, a vibrant dance,
In swirling currents, a fleeting chance.
With every flick, a story told,
In rhythms of the brave and bold.

Like lullabies from murky deep,
The echoes stir, as creatures leap.
Here, in the bower, hearts entwine,
With every splash, the stars align.

So listen close, to nature's song,
In watery realms, we all belong.
For in this haven, dreams take flight,
And harmonies, will guide the night.

Frayed Threads of Celestial Currents

In twilight's weave, the currents flow,
Threads of stars that flicker slow.
Hidden paths through depths unfold,
A tapestry of tales retold.

The cosmos dances, light and shade,
A celestial quilt in darkness made.
With every whisper, secrets unwind,
In ancient threads, our fates aligned.

From the silence, echoes rise,
Of wandering souls beneath the skies.
With frayed edges and shimmering hints,
They stitch the night in twinkling prints.

Through veils of time, the currents wind,
Entwined within, the ties that bind.
A celestial map, a lost refrain,
To guide the heart through joy and pain.

So navigate with tender care,
For in those threads, a love laid bare.
And in each turn, the stars will guide,
Through frayed currents, we shall abide.

The Labyrinth of the Abyssal Garden

In shadowed depths, a garden grows,
Where luminescent secrets pose.
A labyrinth of life, a hidden space,
Where every turn reveals a face.

With twisting paths and soft embrace,
The abyssal blooms take their place.
In silence deep, the voices hum,
A chorus sung where few have come.

The anemones sway, like dancers lost,
In gentle tides, at any cost.
They weave through dreams in swirling light,
Mysterious wonders that ignite.

So wander slow, through this green maze,
Where time dissolves in awe and praise.
Embrace the echoes, fear no end,
For in the garden, we all transcend.

And as you tread this sacred ground,
In depths where mystery is found,
Remember well, the heart's desire,
For in the abyss, we all conspire.

Liquid Whispers of the Deep Blue

In oceans deep where shadows dwell,
The liquid whispers cast a spell.
Beneath the waves, a world untold,
In secrets dark, the mermaids fold.

With silver fins and braided hair,
They glide through currents, unaware.
Each ripple sings of lore and morn,
In depths of blue, their tales are born.

The gentle sway of ocean's sigh,
Calls forth the dreams that dare to fly.
In cerulean realms, the echoes play,
As moonlight weaves the night to day.

A tapestry of currents twine,
Their stories spun, a fate divine.
With every ebb, a heart will yearn,
For whispers sweet, in tides we learn.

The waves they dance, a soft embrace,
Inviting souls to find their place.
In liquid whispers, truths align,
In every pulse, a love's design.

The Siren's Spell of Interlacing Waves

Amidst the foam, a haunting tune,
Where every note brings hearts in swoon.
The siren sings from rocks so high,
With interlacing waves that sigh.

Her voice, a charm that beckons near,
A melody both sweet and clear.
With every lilt, a sailor dreams,
In ocean's grasp, the starlight beams.

Temptation dances on the shore,
As waves entangle, hearts explore.
A song of love, a barren fate,
In siren's grip, they hesitate.

Yet wrapped in tides, the truth will shine,
For every heart, a soul divine.
The ebb and flow, a fierce caress,
In woven song, we find our bliss.

The ocean's arms will hold you tight,
As sirens sing beneath the night.
In interlacing waves, you'll find,
A love that's lost yet so entwined.

Mysteries of the Underwater Loom

In shadows deep, a loom resides,
With threads of fate, the ocean hides.
In currents swift, the weaver knits,
The tapestry of dreams and splits.

A swirling dance of color bright,
Elusive forms drift out of sight.
Each strand a tale, from past to now,
A secret bind, a sacred vow.

In ripples worn, the stories blend,
Of sailors brave who dare to fend.
With every weave, a life is born,
In silent depths, we tread forlorn.

The ocean hums its timeless tune,
A weaver's heart beneath the moon.
The mysteries of the depths unveil,
As whispers linger, touch the veil.

Through ancient tides, the craft persists,
A rhythm found in ocean's mist.
The loom of night, a guiding star,
In every pulse, we've wandered far.

Tidal Threads of Fate

With every tide that sweeps the shore,
A thread unwinds, a tale of lore.
In surging waves, the fates align,
As whispers echo, entwined design.

The moon commands a dance so bold,
As stories old in currents fold.
With hearts adrift, we seek our place,
In tidal threads, our dreams embrace.

Each ebb and flow a chance to weave,
The lives we touch, the love we cleave.
In ocean's grasp, we find our thread,
In tides of fate, our hopes are fed.

A tapestry of ebbing light,
Guides wayward hearts through starry night.
As every splash recalls a name,
In tidal threads, we fuel the flame.

So heed the call of whispers deep,
In ocean's hold, our secrets keep.
With every tide, a tale unfolds,
In threads of fate, our lives are told.

The Looping Song of Currents

In the depths where the shadows play,
Whispers of water dance and sway,
Tales of the tides, lost in the blue,
Echoing secrets, both ancient and new.

A ripple of memories, softly they sing,
Stories of sailors and dreams on the wing,
Carried away by the winding stream,
Drifting through realms, just like a dream.

The currents weave tales in silver and gold,
Of places forgotten and legends retold,
Each wave a chapter in the ocean's refrain,
An endless duet of joy and of pain.

With the moon as the muse, the stars as the guide,
The melody flows like the ebbing tide,
Voices of mariners, long since at sea,
Sing to the soul of the deep and the free.

So listen, dear wanderer, heed the soft call,
For the water remembers, it holds us all,
In the loop of the currents, together we'll roam,
A timeless adventure, the ocean our home.

Enigma of the Nautical Embrace

Beneath the waves where shadows glide,
Lies a realm where the mysteries hide,
With whispers and wonders, a haunting embrace,
Of spirits entwined in the ocean's own grace.

In twilight's shimmer, the sea's gentle sigh,
Unfolds the tales of a ship lost to sky,
With sails in the wind, and hearts full of hope,
They danced with the stars, learned the art of the scope.

The enigma speaks in the currents so fine,
A lover's embrace where the water aligns,
Tangled in rapture, the depths pull us near,
In each salty kiss, the ocean draws dear.

With shells of old stories held close to the chest,
The beauty of darkness becomes our behest,
A symphony swells like the tide rising high,
In the balm of the sea, we whisper goodbye.

For the ocean, it holds us, as only it can,
A portrait of puzzles, a life without plan,
In the nautical love, we surrender in bliss,
In the waves of eternity, a timeless abyss.

Patterns of the Abyssal Bloom

In the silent depths of the deep sea floor,
Life springs forth in colors, a vibrant decor,
Nature's own canvas, with rhythms so rare,
In patterns that twist, like a dance in the air.

Luminescent creatures, aglow in the night,
Choreographed wonders, in water's own light,
Each bloom a reminder, a story proclaimed,
Of life in the darkness, beautifully framed.

The Abyssal Bloom wakes when the world is asleep,
A magical secret the ocean will keep,
With petals like waves, and fragrances bold,
The mystery blossoms, a treasure to hold.

Through currents and shadows, they silently sway,
As currents of blue turn to shades of gray,
Their delicate dance, a mesmerizing sight,
Bringing forth legends in the depth of the night.

From the whispers of water to the tales of the gloom,
The universe breathes in the essence of bloom,
In the depths we discover, a wonder so sweet,
That patterns of life in the ocean repeat.

The Bindings of Ocean's Heart

In a cradle of salt where the sea meets the sky,
Lies a bond so profound, it can never say die,
With each rhythmic wave, a promise is made,
In the stillness of waters, our fears start to fade.

The heart of the ocean beats strong and true,
Its pulse intertwined with the thoughts of the blue,
With treasures of old on the seabed they lie,
Lost fragments of love as the tide rolls by.

The bindings, invisible, strong as the night,
Hold us together in darkness and light,
A journey of souls that the sea has designed,
Where currents and heartstrings are endlessly twined.

With whispers of longing that flow through the tides,
We find comfort in knowing the ocean abides,
In the depths of our dreams, we'll forever remain,
The ocean's sweet heart, through pleasure and pain.

So embrace every wave, let the body be free,
For the bindings of ocean will carry thee,
In the song of the waters, the heart will ignite,
In the dance of the seas, we're lost to the night.

The Call of the Deep

In shadows where the waters sigh,
Mysteries beckon from the brine,
Voices whisper through the tide,
Secrets waiting to entwine.

The moonlit dance of silver streams,
Echoes of a time untold,
Crashing waves, the wildest dreams,
Beneath the depths, where wonders fold.

A siren's song, both sharp and sweet,
Calls with the pull of moonlit grace,
Hearts entwined in rhythmic beat,
Lost in the ocean's warm embrace.

Fathoms deep, where shadows play,
Woven threads of ancient lore,
As tides of time slowly decay,
An endless yearning to explore.

From coral palaces so grand,
To sunken ships of yesteryear,
The deep's allure, a guiding hand,
Awakens dreams, dispels all fear.

Interwoven

In the fabric of the night,
Stars glimmer in the velvet sky,
Threads of fate entwined and bright,
Whispers of a love so nigh.

Across the fields where shadows creep,
Weaving patterns rich and old,
In every dream, our memories keep,
Stories of a heart turned bold.

Hand in hand through paths unknown,
Each step a mark of destiny,
In every tear, the seeds are sown,
A tapestry of you and me.

Threads of laughter, silken ties,
A dance of joy in twilight's hum,
Beneath the watchful, twinkling eyes,
Our interwoven hearts succumb.

In every stitch, a soft embrace,
We forge our bond in gentle light,
A journey shared, a sacred space,
In love's sweet weave, our souls take flight.

Tides of Entangled Yearning

Beneath the waves, where dreams collide,
A dance of longing, soft and wild,
Each ebb and flow a secret guide,
To shores where hope is gently piled.

The salty breeze, a lover's sigh,
As currents pull on hearts undone,
In ocean's arms, we learn to fly,
Two wanderers beneath the sun.

With every dawn, a promise made,
The tide embraces, holds us near,
In tangled depths, we're not afraid,
To lose ourselves, to shed a tear.

The moonlit path, a silken thread,
Leading us to where we belong,
In every wave, a wish is bred,
In every heartbeat, ocean's song.

And as we drift on waters vast,
Entangled in a dance divine,
We share the future and the past,
Two souls adrift in love's design.

Weaves of Wonder Within the Waves

In whispered tides, where shadows play,
The ocean's heart begins to sing,
With every crest, a dream awakes,
A tapestry of wonder brings.

We wander through the endless blue,
With eyes aglow, the starlight glints,
In every ripple, stories brew,
As magic weaves and softly hints.

With coral crowns and seafoam grace,
We dive into the depths unseen,
In every pulse, a hidden space,
A woven world, both rich and green.

Through kelp and shells, we trace the lines,
Of ancient songs in vibrant hues,
In every grain, a treasure shines,
A paradise that we peruse.

As waves embrace the shore's warm sand,
The dance of wonder bids us stay,
To find the magic, hand in hand,
In weaves of wonder, lost in play.

Coral Verses Amidst the Tides

In the twilight glow of the sea,
Coral secrets dance with glee.
Whispered tales from creatures bright,
Swaying softly, heart to light.

Beneath the waves, they weave their song,
Echoing where the brave belong.
A tapestry of colors rare,
Lies hidden in the salt-kissed air.

With every pulse, the ocean sways,
Rhythms born from ancient days.
Fragile beauty, poised and free,
Lives in depths of mystery.

In twilight's arms, they find their peace,
Each gentle wave a sweet release.
Coral verses, soft and true,
Tell of worlds that we once knew.

As moonlight spills on ocean's face,
Time stands still in this embrace.
Nature's whispers, a sacred guide,
Awake the dreams the tides confide.

The Enigma Beneath the Surface

In silence deep, where shadows lie,
An enigma stirs, beneath the sigh.
Hidden realms with secrets old,
Unfurling stories yet untold.

With every current, whispers blend,
A timeless riddle without end.
Lost in depths, a treasure waits,
In the heart where time abates.

Figures loom in the mirage light,
Fleeting as day surrenders night.
Mysteries weave through watery veils,
Painting castles in the gales.

Bubbles carrying the dreams of yore,
Echo through the ocean's lore.
Dancers twirl in fluid grace,
Eternal secrets to embrace.

In shadows thick, the truth will gleam,
Lost in the solitude of stream.
The enigma calls, it cannot stay,
Yet guides the heart along its way.

Lament of the Tidebound Spirit

A spirit wanders by the shore,
Bound by tides forevermore.
Echoes of a distant past,
Yearning for a home at last.

Whispers of the sea complain,
Sorrow wrapped in misty rain.
Every wave a heavy sigh,
Carrying dreams that drift and die.

In the moonlight, shadows creep,
Lost in dreams, the spirit weeps.
Unfinished tales ride the swell,
A haunting voice, a silent bell.

Yet within the storm's embrace,
Lies a flicker of sweet grace.
Hope may rise with the morning tide,
To heal the heart where sorrow resides.

So let the waves their story bear,
Carrying the burdened air.
For every lament, a hero's quest,
In tides that hold the heart's true rest.

Threads of Enchantment in the Deep

In the depths where shadows dwell,
Threads of magic weave a spell.
Creatures twirl in silken streams,
Crafting wonder from their dreams.

Dancing through the sunlit beams,
Whispers rise like moonlit gleams.
Fins adorned in jeweled hue,
Unravel stories ever new.

Coral kingdoms hold their breath,
Embracing life, defying death.
Every heartbeat in the sea,
Weaves the fabric of the free.

Enchanted waters hum a song,
A melody where all belong.
Echoing through caverns bold,
Secrets waiting to be told.

And in these depths, where dreams take flight,
The threads of life illuminate the night.
A tapestry of sea and soul,
Binding all, making us whole.

Wistful Currents of Uncharted Depths

In shadows deep where whispers roam,
A hidden dream, a distant home.
Beneath the waves, a story sleeps,
In currents swift, the history keeps.

The moonlight dances, soft and pale,
On silent ships that tell the tale.
Of sailors lost in yearning's grip,
With every tide, their hearts still sip.

The ocean's breath, a siren's call,
It weaves a spell, enchanting all.
Through tempest wild and tranquil night,
The depths hold secrets, cloaked in light.

Each wave that crashes, speaks a song,
Of journeys vast, both right and wrong.
In watery halls where dreams entwine,
The heart of earth, both kind and divine.

So let us sail on azure streams,
With the compass set towards our dreams.
For every tide, a chance to find,
The treasures spun by fate entwined.

The Interwoven Secrets of Sea and Sky

Above the waves, the seagulls soar,
While down below, tales whisper more.
A tapestry of blue and gold,
In every hue, a story told.

The sky ignites with dusk's embrace,
As stars emerge, a shining lace.
Reflecting on the ocean's face,
The secrets mingle, hidden grace.

In breezes soft, the echoes sigh,
Of ancient lore that won't say die.
The sailor's heart, the dreamer's muse,
In uninhibited paths, we choose.

The storms may rage, yet hope remains,
In every loss, a wealth of gains.
For nature's pulse, both fierce and kind,
Weaving the threads of heart and mind.

So let us sail 'neath starlit skies,
Embrace the winds, let spirits rise.
For in this dance of sea and air,
The pulse of life, beyond compare.

Echoes of a Fabric Collage Below

In depths obscure, old voices stir,
Through fragments lost, we softly purr.
A fabric woven of dreams and tears,
Whispers of time through endless years.

The coral blooms in colors bright,
As shadows play in a soft twilight.
Each stitch, a moment stitched with care,
Echoing softly, a tender prayer.

The minnows dart in playful grace,
While currents weave in a soft embrace.
Every ripple a soft refrain,
A melody lost, but not in vain.

The ocean breathes, a living art,
With every wave, it plays its part.
A story woven in beads of light,
Where day meets night, and wrong finds right.

So listen close and you might hear,
The echoes whispering from afar.
In the collage of lives below,
The heart keeps beating; love will grow.

Tides that Bind and Unravel

The tides arise, a rhythmic dance,
In every wave, a fleeting chance.
They bind our hearts, yet tear away,
In liquid whispers of the day.

Each crest and trough, a tale unfolds,
Of love once warm now turning cold.
Yet through the storm, we find our way,
For tides may change, but hearts will stay.

In silvered light, the moon shines bright,
Casting its glow on the lonely night.
With every pull, we drift apart,
But still, the ocean holds our heart.

In every ebb, a chance to grow,
Though loss may sting, the love will flow.
We rise with dawn, and fall with dusk,
In oceans deep, in dreams we trust.

So let us sail on changing seas,
With hopes afloat on every breeze.
For tides will bind and gently lead,
The heart's true journey, indeed.

Labors of Love in the Silent Depths

In shadows deep where whispers tread,
The heart's soft echoes linger near.
With gentle hands, the dreams are spread,
For love's sweet labor knows no fear.

Beneath the waves, where secrets lay,
A bond is sewn in silky seams.
Each pulse a rhythm, night and day,
We craft our life from floating dreams.

In silence, words begin to dance,
In moonlit pools where visions bloom.
Our tender wishes in a glance,
Unravel shadows, chase the gloom.

Together bound, we brave the tide,
In depths where joy and sorrow blend.
With steadfast hearts, we shall abide,
For love, once found, will never end.

The silent depths, a canvas wide,
With brushstrokes bold and colors bright.
In labors of love, we confide,
Crafting our dreams in softest light.

Fables Embedded in the Abyss

In depths where ancient stories weave,
Fables lost in time's embrace.
Whispers of dreams, the tales believe,
In darkened waters, find their place.

The echoes call from sunken lore,
Where mermaids sing and shadows play.
Each fable holds a hidden door,
To worlds where night consumes the day.

With every current, secrets churn,
Beneath the waves, the truths unfold.
In silence deep, we yearn and learn,
As ages pass, our hearts grow bold.

In coral groves, a map concealed,
With riddles wrapped in mystic hues.
The ocean's heart, a voice revealed,
In fables told, our sorrow soothes.

Yet caution beckons, tread with care,
For not all tales are light and warm.
The darkness hides with subtle flair,
And fables lurk in every storm.

The Intertwining of Water and Yearning

In twilight's touch, the river flows,
With yearning hearts that brave the stream.
The dance of water softly glows,
Reflecting all that we can dream.

Beneath our aching, restless souls,
The current calls us ever near.
In liquid paths, our spirit rolls,
A gentle nudge, a quiet cheer.

Each droplet holds a tale untold,
Of passion deep and whispered pain.
With every wave, the memories fold,
Into the tide, we're bound again.

Yet in the depths, we find that spark,
The light of hope against the dark.
With yearning pure, we chase the mark,
The intertwining, water's arc.

Together we shall brave the flow,
In harmony, our spirits rise.
For love's sweet song, we shall bestow,
In every wave, our hearts' reprise.

Riddles Wrapped in Coral Colors

In gardens deep where colors gleam,
Riddles whisper in the breeze.
Coral wonders shape the dream,
Inviting hearts to roam with ease.

Each hue a question, bright and bold,
An ocean's puzzle waits to solve.
In beauty's grasp, our secrets hold,
As waves of wonder softly evolve.

With every flash, the world unveils,
A tapestry of sea and sky.
Wrapped in riddles, truth prevails,
As coral shadows drift and fly.

Yet navigators must take care,
For hidden dangers lie in wait.
Within the colors, unaware,
The heart may find its kindred fate.

So let us sail on waters bright,
With courage sturdy in our sails.
Through riddles wrapped in coral light,
We'll journey forth, where hope prevails.

The Song Weavers of the Deep Blue

In the depths where shadows play,
The song weavers weave, night and day.
With whispers of currents, soft and low,
They craft the tales of ebb and flow.

From coral gardens, vibrant and bright,
They serenade the moon's silver light.
Each note a treasure from the sea bed,
A melody spun where secrets are fed.

Their voices dance like waves in the breeze,
Calling the creatures with effortless ease.
In the blue, where the tickling tides amuse,
They sing of dreams that the ocean imbues.

Through kelp forests, their symphonies roam,
Filling the waters, making it home.
A harmony of colors, rich and warm,
In the deep, they create a soft balm.

So listen close when the ocean calls,
To the song weavers beneath the stalls.
For every note carries a wish, a plea,
In the heart of the deep blue, wild and free.

Echoes of Love in the Marine Abyss

Beneath the waves, where silence weeps,
Echoes of love in the darkness creeps.
With each soft ripple, a promise made,
In the marine abyss, memories cascade.

The gentle sway of aquatic dreams,
Floating softly on moonlit beams.
Starfish embrace the sands below,
As whispers of lovers stir the flow.

In the shadows, secrets entwine,
Linking hearts in a dance divine.
The ocean's breath carries the sighs,
Of souls that found each other, 'neath the skies.

Glistening shells share tales of grace,
Moments cherished in time's embrace.
As dolphins leap with joyous calls,
Their laughter echoes through watery halls.

So dive deep where the heartbeats throng,
In the depths of love, we all belong.
Within the marine abyss, pure and bright,
The echoes of love hold the stars at night.

A Tangle of Seashell Memories

On the shore where soft winds sigh,
A tangle of seashell memories lie.
Each shell a story, a whisper, a call,
Of waves that danced and began to fall.

Their colors gleam in the sun's warm gaze,
Reflecting the ocean's magical haze.
With each gentle touch, a past comes alive,
In the seashell's curve, dreams do thrive.

The tides remember, they ebb and flow,
Carrying secrets only they know.
With every heartbeat, a memory flows,
In the gathering mist, where the sea breeze blows.

Among the treasures of wonder and time,
Each seashell keeps a rhythm, a rhyme.
Holding the laughter of children at play,
And whispers of lovers at the end of the day.

So gather the seashells, hold them dear,
For in their presence, time's echo is clear.
In a tangle of memories, we find our way,
Through the sands of the shore, come what may.

Weaving Dreams in Liquid Silk

In the twilight where shadows blend,
We weave our dreams, a tale to send.
Liquid silk flows from the heart's embrace,
Creating magic in a timeless space.

The ocean's surface, a canvas wide,
Where wishes float and daydreams glide.
With every ripple, visions take flight,
In the depths of dream, all feels right.

In the currents that hum, let worries cease,
For beneath the waves, we find our peace.
Starlit patterns dance like fireflies,
In the realm of dreams, the spirit flies.

As the tides caress the shores of night,
We spin our hopes with gentle light.
Each thread a promise, soft as a sigh,
In liquid silk, our hearts can fly.

So dive where the dreams are spun anew,
In the shimmering depths of a magical hue.
With each whispered thought, let the journey start,
Weaving dreams in liquid silk, heart to heart.

The Siren's Twisted Embrace

In twilight's glow, a haunting call,
A melody that doth enthrall.
Waves lap softly against the shore,
A promise whispered, forevermore.

With hair like seaweed, dark and sly,
She beckons sailors doomed to fly.
Her laughter dances on the breeze,
A siren's charm, a heart in freeze.

The tides reveal her chilling form,
In waters deep, where dreams transform.
The shipwrecked dreams on jagged rocks,
Lie tangled in those treacherous docks.

Yet hope remains, a flickering light,
For those who dare to brave the night.
With courage forged from moonlit grace,
They seek the truth in her embrace.

But heed the tale of those who've gone,
The siren's song, a deadly dawn.
In twisted fate, her laughter fades,
As shadows claim the sunlit glades.

Seashells Entangled in Time

Upon the shore, where whispers dwell,
Lie seashells cast, with tales to tell.
Their spiraled forms, a map of days,
In ocean's grip, in sunlight's rays.

Each shell a memory, bright and bold,
Of tides that danced, of legends told.
An echo soft from ages past,
In grains of sand, their shadows cast.

With every wave, a secret spent,
A silence deep, a wonderment.
What dreams reside within the shell,
What stories from the ocean swell?

And as the moon draws forth the deep,
The oceans sigh, the waters weep.
A treasure found, a heart confined,
In seashells' embrace, all mixed in time.

So listen close, when storms arise,
For in the shells, the world replies.
Their twinkling tones shall guide your way,
Through fleeting nights and dawning day.

Mysteries of the Deep Blue Braid

Beneath the waves, a secret lies,
In tangled strands where silence flies.
The deep blue braid of ocean's lore,
Holds mysteries we long ignore.

With every ripple, whispers grow,
Of sunken ships, of tales untold.
The spirits linger, lost in song,
In currents where the heart belongs.

A net of dreams, a weave so fine,
Entwined with fate, the cross of time.
In depths unknown, the heart can drown,
In azure twilight, slips the crown.

Yet brave the souls who seek the light,
Who venture forth to face the night.
For in the depths, the truth is bound,
In watery graves, where hopes are found.

So delve into the ocean's fold,
Where every wave unravels gold.
In mysteries that nature spawns,
The deep blue braid forever dawns.

Ocean's Lament: A Tidal Knot

The ocean wails, a mournful sound,
As tides collide on rocky ground.
In shadows cast by moonlit grace,
It weaves a tale of dreams displaced.

The salty air, a heavy breath,
In every wave, a song of death.
Yet in the storm, there's beauty rare,
A dance of grief in salty air.

Beneath the foam, the secrets lie,
Where whispers fade and shadows sigh.
A tidal knot, a sailor's plight,
Entwined in fog, lost from the light.

But still the ocean finds its way,
Through ebb and flow, by night and day.
For every tear that falls as rain,
Is washed ashore, then born again.

In nature's grip, we find our place,
A fleeting glimpse of endless space.
The ocean's lament, a song well-known,
In tides that pull the heart and bone.

Tangled Vines of Ocean Dreams

In twilight's hush, the sea begins,
Where tangled vines, the journey spins.
They dance with whispers of the night,
Embracing shadows, soft and light.

Beneath the waves, where secrets hide,
A melody of dreams, a tide.
The light that glimmers, bright and clear,
Calls to the souls, both far and near.

Around each curve, the stories flow,
Of ancient paths and hearts that glow.
The moonlight weaves a silver lace,
Enfolding all in sea's embrace.

With every breath, the currents sigh,
And paint the sky where mermaids fly.
A tapestry of colors bold,
In marine tales, forever told.

So let the ocean's wonders gleam,
In tangled vines of every dream.
For in the depths, our spirits glide,
Through realms of magic, side by side.

Secrets Woven in Salty Waves

The ocean breathes a secret song,
In salty waves, where spirits throng.
Each ripple holds a tale untold,
A treasure chest of legends old.

The starfish pause, the seagrass sways,
Beneath the sun's warm, golden rays.
A gentle nudge from fate's kind hand,
Guides wandering hearts to wonderland.

Oceans churn with laughter, glee,
Where dreams are free and spirits flee.
In every splash, a wish is spun,
Beneath the light of setting sun.

The tides may shift, the storms may roar,
Yet whispers linger on the shore.
In each drop of rain from skies above,
Lives the rhythm of ocean love.

So listen close, let silence weave,
The secrets that the seas conceive.
With every wave, a promise made,
In salty depths where dreams cascade.

Enchanted Loops Beneath the Tide

In enchanted loops, the currents swirl,
With each soft pulse, the oceans whirl.
The water glimmers with a spell,
Where hidden wonders softly dwell.

Anemones sway with grace divine,
In gentle touch where colors shine.
A world aglow with magic steeped,
In depths where dreams are safely kept.

The seahorses dance in joyous flight,
Beneath the moon's soft, silver light.
A mystical realm of whispers found,
In the heartbeats of the ocean sound.

Coral gardens, vibrant and bright,
Ripple with life, a painted sight.
Among the seaweed, secrets bloom,
Enchanted loops, a sacred room.

For every wave that laps the shore,
Holds tales of yore, forevermore.
In this embrace, lost souls reside,
In enchanted loops beneath the tide.

Whispers of the Coral Sanctuary

In coral sanctuaries, whispers call,
With every tide, they rise and fall.
A colorful realm, so vibrant, rare,
Where magic lingers in the air.

The fish weave tales in playful streams,
In shimmering hues of distant dreams.
Beneath the waves, a home so bright,
Filled with the love of day and night.

Upon the reef, where sunbeams play,
The ocean speaks in a gentle sway.
With every crest, the heartbeats dance,
In rhythm with the waves' advance.

The octopus hides with artful grace,
In crevices, a secret space.
Each moment glows with life anew,
In whispers soft, the ocean's cue.

So dive into this sacred place,
Where time slows down, and fears erase.
For in the depths, we find our way,
In whispers of the coral sway.

Trapped in the Seafoam's Whimsy

Beneath the waves where secrets dwell,
The seafoam swirls, casting its spell.
Ghostly whispers ride the tide,
In dreams of sailors lost, they bide.

A mermaid's song floats through the air,
Weaving tales of joy and despair.
Tangled in the nets of fate,
They drift along, forever wait.

Each bubble bursts with a playful cheer,
Yet hides the sorrow, laced with fear.
For those who hear the ocean sigh,
Shall know the truth of anchor's tie.

Luminous grains tell of the past,
Memories in the waves are cast.
Ah, but the sea, it keeps its might,
In shadows deep, far from the light.

So if you stand 'neath moonlit skies,
And feel the pull as twilight flies,
Know that you're caught in whimsy's dance,
A fleeting touch of fate, a chance.

The Ocean's Lament for Forgotten Shores

The tides roll in with mourning grace,
Beneath a sky of clouded lace.
Once vibrant sands, now faded dreams,
Echoes lost in silent screams.

Faded footprints washed away,
Whispers of children gone astray.
Seagulls cry their hollow tune,
For sunlit days, now gone too soon.

The driftwood tells of ships long gone,
Of battles fought at dawn's first yawn.
Yet here we stand, the past to bear,
While wild winds weave a tale of care.

Each wave a tear, each splash a sigh,
As if the ocean yearns to cry.
For every soul that loved these shores,
The deep keeps watch, as beauty roars.

And though the sands may slip away,
The heart remembers every day.
In whispered dreams, the sea shall call,
A longing that binds us, one and all.

Symphonic Currents of the Abyss

In depths where light can seldom tread,
A symphony of shadows spread.
Currents swirl like notes in flight,
A ballet danced in endless night.

The giants roam, both fierce and grand,
In this dark realm, they make their stand.
Each thrum and pulse tells tales of yore,
Of battles fought on an ancient shore.

The echoing calls of creatures fair,
Resound in silence, kiss the air.
Notes of the deep, both sweet and dire,
In heart and soul, they weave desire.

With every tide a story grows,
Of love, of loss, as the ocean flows.
So listen close to the abyss's song,
For therein lies where hearts belong.

As mermaids spin their tales of woe,
The currents flow, an endless show.
In symphonic waves, let spirits soar,
The depths entwined, forevermore.

Garland of Fables in Ocean's Caress

In ocean's cradle, stories weave,
Of fables whispered, none believe.
A garland strung on waves that flow,
Binds tales of joy with hints of woe.

Naiads weave their shimmering thread,
In twilight's glow, where legends tread.
Each drop a tale, both bold and bright,
Of lovers lost, of day and night.

The salt-kissed air, the foam that swirls,
Holds secrets wrapped in tender pearls.
In every shell, a world concealed,
A promise made, a hope revealed.

As fishermen cast their nets of dreams,
They pull the sea's most silvered beams.
With laughter bright, they gather round,
In unity where joy is found.

So let the ocean's tales embrace,
With gentle touch, a warm embrace.
For in its depths, the heart shall see,
A garland of fables, wild and free.

The Symphony of Ensnared Hearts

In twilight's glow, the whispers start,
Silent notes that draw the heart.
Each longing glance, a hidden tune,
A dance beneath the silver moon.

With every sigh, a promise made,
In shadows deep, our love displayed.
Bound by fate, together we sway,
In harmony, we'll find our way.

A melody of dreams, so bright,
Entwined beneath the fading light.
A symphony, both soft and clear,
In every beat, I draw you near.

Yet tempests rage beyond our shore,
Each heartbeat calls for something more.
But in this song, our souls unite,
In every challenge, we find light.

So let us dream, just you and I,
With lullabies that never die.
In this enchanted world of art,
We'll weave forever, heart to heart.

Currents of Enchantment

Beneath the waves where secrets swell,
Currents weave a timeless spell.
Each ripple hums a tale of old,
Of love's embrace, both fierce and bold.

In twilight's grasp, the stars align,
A world unseen, your heart in mine.
With whispered wishes on the breeze,
Our souls entwined, like swaying trees.

The tides of fate, they pull us close,
In every swell, my heart engrossed.
With every shift, we chart our course,
In tranquil depths, we find our force.

The moon casts light on waters deep,
Where dreams and shadows softly creep.
In currents strong, our spirits flow,
A dance of love that none can slow.

So let us sail, past shores unseen,
On waves of joy, where hearts convene.
In every surge, let passion rise,
In this vast sea, we'll claim our prize.

Woven Together

In silver threads, our lives entwine,
Each moment's stitch, a gift divine.
With laughter bright, and tears of grace,
We forge our bond in time and space.

Through storms that come and skies that clear,
In woven dreams, we persevere.
Each fabric hug, a warm embrace,
In every touch, a sacred place.

The tapestry of love we weave,
With colors bold, we must believe.
In every choice, a pattern spun,
A journey shared, not just for one.

So let the threads of fate combine,
In every heart, a story line.
Together strong, we'll face the fight,
For love's embrace is pure delight.

With every stitch, a bond we share,
In woven dreams, we'll find our air.
Forever stitched, our fates conjoin,
In love's great quilt, we will enjoin.

The Nautical Gardens of Uncertainty

In gardens deep beneath the tides,
Where hidden wonders gently hide,
A world unfolds, both strange and bright,
In whispers soft, we seek the light.

The sea holds tales of love's embrace,
In tangled roots, we find our place.
With every wave, the sands may shift,
Yet in this dance, we find our gift.

Each flower blooms, a fleeting chance,
As tides may turn, we learn to dance.
In storms that rise, we stand our ground,
In uncertainty, love's strength is found.

So let the waters guide our way,
In nautical gardens, come what may.
Through every current, we will strive,
For in our hearts, true love will thrive.

And in this realm where hope takes flight,
We'll nurture dreams with all our might.
For even in the depths of doubt,
Our hearts will sing, of this no doubt.

Love Knots Beneath the Waves

Down where the ocean's whispers flow,
Live love knots only we can know.
Entangled hearts in depths of blue,
A bond that's rare, forever true.

With every tide, our roots take hold,
In secret groves, our stories told.
A silent oath in currents deep,
In ocean's cradle, dreams to keep.

So when the storms should dare to rise,
We'll brave the winds, with steady eyes.
For in each wave that breaks and falls,
Our love shall echo through the halls.

With treasures found on sandy shores,
We'll write our tale, by ancient oars.
In darkened depths, where shadows cling,
Our love's sweet song will always sing.

For every knot, a tale to share,
In love's embrace, we find our rare.
So let the sea and stars align,
In every tide, your heart is mine.

Tides of Enchantment in a Spiral

In whispered echoes, secrets flow,
Beneath the tides, where wonders grow.
A spiral dance of moonlit glow,
Where mermaids sing and breezes blow.

Among the shells, a magic bright,
A world awash in pure delight.
With every wave, the stars ignite,
In dreams of deep and endless night.

In currents strong, the heart's embrace,
A gentle pull, a timeless chase.
In oceans vast, we find our place,
Together bound, no need for space.

The salt of love, the spray of tears,
Against the dark, it calms our fears.
With every tide, our vision clears,
A song that lingers through the years.

So let us sail on waves of fate,
With hearts entwined, we won't be late.
In spirals spun, we'll celebrate,
The tides of love, our wondrous state.

Ribbons of Light in Aquatic Shadows

In depths where shadows softly gleam,
Ribbons of light weave through a dream.
They shimmer bright, a silver stream,
Awakening the soul's deep theme.

With finned companions by our side,
We swim through wonders, hearts open wide.
In aquatic realms, where secrets bide,
The waves embrace, our fears subside.

Glimmers dance 'neath the surface blue,
A canvas painted, fresh and new.
Where whispers and laughter, light breaks through,
In every corner, magic's due.

With every ripple, stories flow,
Of ancient tales, lost long ago.
In twilight's kiss, the currents know,
A grand adventure, let's go slow.

So join me now, in this mystique,
Dive beneath, let hearts not peak.
With ribbons bright, our spirits speak,
In shadows dance, where dreams aren't bleak.

Whirling Vortex of Love and Mystery

A whirling vortex pulls us near,
Where love and mystery appear.
In swirling depths, no need for fear,
As hearts collide, the path is clear.

Through tempests wild, we find our way,
With every turn, we learn to sway.
In swirling arms, we softly lay,
Embraced by night, eclipsed by day.

The tide of fate, it twists and bends,
In swirling minds, the journey sends.
From depths unknown, our magic blends,
In dreams of twilight, love transcends.

In every whirl, a spark ignites,
Through great unknowns, our souls take flight.
From shadows cast, to shimmering lights,
In endless dance, we chase the nights.

So take my hand, let's spiral down,
Into the whirl, we'll wear our crowns.
In vortex strong, where joy abounds,
Our hearts unite, true love resounds.

Veils of Dreams in Ocean's Grasp

In veils of dreams, we softly tread,
Where whispers of the ocean spread.
The tides unveil what's long since said,
In depths sublime, where hearts are led.

Through silken currents, softly sway,
In ocean's grasp, we find our way.
The dreams arise, they dance, they play,
In every wave, our troubles lay.

With each new tide, the past will shift,
In waters deep, the spirits lift.
From shadows cast, we find the gift,
In every breath, our souls uplift.

So let us weave through liquid gold,
In gentle grasp, with love so bold.
In dreams of old, the stories told,
In ocean's heart, our fate unfolds.

Together bound, through sea and sky,
In veils of dreams, with every sigh.
In endless blue, we'll soar and fly,
With ocean's love, we'll never die.

Lured by the Currents of the Unknown

Beneath the waves where shadows play,
A siren's call, a whispered sway.
The deep blue beckons, secrets weave,
Adventures linger, so hard to believe.

Starlit dreams in foamy embrace,
Mermaids dance in hidden space.
Every ripple, a tale untold,
Where mysteries stir in currents bold.

The ocean breathes, a sigh most sweet,
With every tide, our hearts it greets.
What lies beyond, we long to find,
In the depths, our souls entwined.

Echoes of laughter, memories soar,
In sunken ships on an ancient shore.
Waves will carry us, lost yet true,
As we venture into the blue.

The current's pull, a magic spell,
Whispers of realms where legends dwell.
We dive into the unknown night,
Our dreams are sails, our hearts alight.

Oceanic Reveries in Twisted Patterns

Waves curl like dreams in a restless sea,
Patterns of whispers, wild and free.
Tides of memory sweep us away,
In spiral dances of night and day.

Seagulls cry above the foam,
Guiding us far from our earthly home.
The ocean's breath, a lullaby,
Calls us forth as stars draw nigh.

Swirls of azure in sunlight's gleam,
Reflect the joy that makes our heart beam.
In the spray, we catch our fate,
Entwined in dreams, we hesitate.

Hidden treasures and whispered lore,
Await beneath the watery floor.
Each crest a window to worlds unknown,
In oceanic whispers, we have grown.

With every surge, the stories blend,
The ocean waits, our loyal friend.
In tranquil depths, we find our peace,
As waves compose our sweet release.

Divinations from the Depths

In somber depths of twilight's gaze,
Secrets linger in ocean's haze.
Crystal orbs of shining light,
Reveal the truth in the cloak of night.

With seashells shout and coral song,
Ancient wisdom whispers strong.
The depths alone hold myriad signs,
In swirling currents, magic aligns.

Visions dance in the briny deep,
Where fish weave dreams that softly seep.
Each flick and flash, a story spun,
In the darkened depths, a fate begun.

The depths hold echoes, past and real,
In knowing tides that twist and reel.
To surf the waves is but a jest,
For within lies the heart's true quest.

As the moon calls forth the ebb and flow,
We seek the wisdom of waters below.
Guided by dreams, through time we thrived,
In ocean's clasp, our souls arrived.

Ocean's Brocade of Ancient Legends

Fables woven in twilight's thread,
Ocean's fabric, where dreams are bred.
From shipwrecked tales of days gone by,
To whispered legends beneath the sky.

Every wave a story spun,
Heroes rise and legends run.
The moonlit sea, a stage of lore,
Cradles mysteries from ages yore.

In kelp forests, shadows delight,
Guardians watch in the moon's soft light.
Tales of sailors lost at sea,
Entwined with merfolk's symphony.

The ocean sings of bygone strife,
Of storms and quests that spark with life.
Each crest and fall, a history told,
Of dreams entwined in waters bold.

In every tide, the old sings new,
Golden threads in the sapphire hue.
The ocean's brocade, endless and wide,
Holds the ancients, our cherished guide.

Charmed by the Siren's Thread

In twilight's glow, a whisper sings,
Of shimmering shells, and hidden things.
A voice that dances on the breeze,
Enticing hearts, like honeyed tease.

With every note, the waters sway,
Drawing souls that drift away.
A tapestry of ancient lore,
Woven deep in ocean's store.

The moonlit waves, a gentle cast,
Holding secrets of the past.
A call so sweet, a haunting plea,
To venture forth, to sail the sea.

In shadows deep, where dreams do dwell,
The siren's song weaves its spell.
With eyes aglow, we heed the tide,
Embracing fate, no place to hide.

And as we swirl in silken strands,
Entwined like seaweed on the sands.
Forever bound in ocean's grace,
Charmed by the siren's sweet embrace.

Seas of Memory Intertwined

Beneath the waves, where echoes lie,
Whispers of dreams that never die.
Shadows cast by moments past,
In memory's embrace, we hold fast.

The ocean floor, a canvas broad,
Painted with tears and laughter's nod.
Every grain of sand retains,
The pulse of love, the taste of pains.

In gentle swells, connection stirs,
The tides of time, like soft-spun furs.
As currents weave through heart and mind,
We find the threads of fate aligned.

These seas of memory intertwine,
Lost in the depths, yet forever shine.
Each wave a tale, each splash a dream,
Together they dance, a timeless theme.

We sail the spheres, both near and far,
Guided by light from a distant star.
Chasing the whispers that call us back,
To shores where echoes never lack.

The Waves Speak in Riddles

Upon the shore, where shadows play,
The waves converse in riddled sway.
Each crash holds secrets, old and new,
Mysteries caught in ocean's hue.

To listen close, to hear them sigh,
A symphony beneath the sky.
In every roll, a tale resides,
Of moonlit dances and hidden tides.

With salt on lips, we ponder deep,
The promises the waters keep.
A rhythm found in heartbeats shared,
A love that's breathed, a bond declared.

Yet riddles twist in every crest,
A game of chance, a fickle jest.
To seek the truth within the foam,
To find the path that leads us home.

The waves, they speak in cryptic song,
Inviting all who dare belong.
A labyrinth of fate and chance,
In every leap, in every dance.

Beneath the Surface: Stories Untold

Beneath the waves, a world concealed,
Where stories whisper, fate revealed.
In twilight hues, the shadows dwell,
Each ripple hides a secret spell.

Sunken dreams on coral beds,
Echoes of words that time has shed.
Fish dart by, like thoughts in flight,
Guardians of the deep, shining bright.

With every tide, a new tale brews,
A song of loss, a dance of blues.
For in the depths, the heart must roam,
As currents pull it far from home.

The kelp sways gently, a curtain drawn,
Revealing glimpses of the dawn.
Of lives entwined, of love's embrace,
As shadows kiss the ocean's face.

So plunge with me, beneath the swell,
In waters where the stories dwell.
Unfurl the threads of time gone by,
And listen close, as echoes sigh.